GRIGORI (

CONCENTRATION EXERCISES

THESE EXERCISES FOR EVERY DAY OF THE MONTH WILL
DEVELOP YOUR CONSCIOUSNESS; THEY WILL INFLUENCE
THE DIRECTION OF YOUR LIFE'S EVENTS IN A POSITIVE WAY;
THEY WILL HELP YOU ACHIEVE PERFECT HEALTH AND BE IN
TUNE WITH THE PULSE OF THE UNIVERSE

HAMBURG
2011

Jelezky publishing, Hamburg
www.jelezky-media.com

1st Edition
First English Edition, December 2011

© 2011 English Language Version
Dimitri Eletski, Hamburg, Germany (Publisher)

For further information on the contents of this book
contact: SVET center, Hamburg, Germany
www.svet-centre.eu

ISBN: 978-3-943110-31-9

Dear Reader,

I recommend that you find time in your daily schedule to acquire the techniques and do the exercises offered below. Three exercises are suggested for each day of the month. These exercises will teach you how to control events in your life by using different concentration techniques. During the process of concentration you should always keep in mind the concrete goal you are trying to achieve. Your goal may consist in bringing about a desired outcome, such as curing a disease, for instance, or developing the tools for cognition of the World, etc. The most important task is to work on regulating information for the benefit of mankind's salvation and harmonious development. This effort may also imply fighting with destruction at the information level, since you undertake here the role of rescuer.

In practice, at the level of your own perception, concentration may be achieved in the following manner:

– Visualize the goal of your concentration efforts as a certain geometrical form, such as a sphere. This is the sphere of the goal indicated in your concentration.

– Compose yourself spiritually to be able to build desired events the same way as the Creator.

– While concentrating on different objects or concrete numbers, or on comprehending reality, you should remain in control of the sphere's location. Use the power of your will to move the sphere into that area of your perception, which radiates more light at the moment of concentration.

I am presenting here only one option of concentration techniques. Many others may be discovered in practice. Methods of controlling events based on understanding World processes through concentration are extremely effective.

In the first exercise for each day of the month you should concentrate on some element of your outer or inner reality.

In the second exercise you should concentrate on a numerical sequence – a seven-digit and then a nine-digit number.

In the third exercise you will find a verbal description of the techniques for controlling life events.

Let me emphasize one very important aspect of the entire training course: you must understand that the effectiveness of your concentration depends primarily on your approach towards it. Do your best to open yourself to this creative process. Listen to your inner voice, as it prompts you on how exactly you should execute these concentration techniques in practice.

As I have already mentioned, one method is to write a sequence of numbers on a piece of paper and concentrate on them. Another approach is also possible.

While concentrating on a sequence of nine numbers, you can try to imagine that you are in the center of a sphere, and the numbers are distributed along its inner surface. You can visualize the information on the goal of your concentration in the shape of a ball that is placed within this sphere. You must focus on identifying which number in the sequence emits more light than the others. At the very first thought that allows you to single out a particular number written on the inner surface of the large sphere

4

as shining brighter than the rest, you should focus your mind just upon this number. You should then mentally connect the inner sphere containing the ball, the goal of the concentration exercise, with the selected element of perception – the most brightly shining number.

When concentrating on a sequence of seven numbers, you can imagine that the numbers are distributed along the outer surface of a cube, on any one of its sides.

Listening to your inner voice you can move the numbers around, changing their location until you reach the maximum effect.

A totally different approach is also possible. You can mentally connect each number with some element in your outer or inner world. Mind you, these elements don't have to be of a similar nature. You may, for instance, associate one number with a tree and another number with some emotion. It is up to you to make the choice. With this method you symbolically equate each number with a chosen element of reality. These elements of reality can always be either physical or mental. This means that they can also be images visualized by your consciousness.

All these techniques will provide you with new avenues for exercising control. You will be at liberty to change the structure of your concentration and your ways of adapting to it. You will also be free to choose from a variety of symbolic equations between the numbers in the sequence and the corresponding elements of reality. This allows you to make your concentration more effective. What is more, you can achieve better control over the amount of time needed to reach your goal, which is of major importance considering the time constraints of everyday life.

Where instantaneous rescue is needed, your concentration must bring immediate results. When the goal lies in finding ways that will guarantee your harmonious development, then the time factor may be less significant. What is important here is to ensure that you are on a path to further your personal harmonious development, while taking all possible circumstances into account. This is precisely what the concentration techniques are meant to accomplish.

As you can see, everything in these exercises and techniques must be adapted to the individual. Everyone should seek out his or her own strategy for personal growth and development. In this regard, it is important to remember the following:

The choice of one's personal self-development strategy cannot be made through logical considerations alone. You undoubtedly set your own goals and do your best to fulfill them, but in your soul there are intended tasks for you that were defined at an earlier time. That is why your concentration exercises and techniques may initially target these earlier tasks, which existed in the soul previously and focused not only on your personal growth and development, but also to the harmonious development of society as a whole. As you fulfill these tasks, you will intuitively sense that this should be your first mission. You will sense it deep inside, at the level of the development of the soul, at the level of the Creator.

And this is the reason why, when referring to concentration, we are above all speaking of universal harmony. Here you must understand that working to establish harmony always presupposes as its essential element the element of rescue and salvation, if the situation is such that it requires such intervention. However, the main task in creating harmony is to secure such a development of events, which will prevent the possibility of a threatening situation. And you should ensure of course that this process of harmonious development is constant and permanent.

The concentration techniques and exercises for each day of the month

6

that I have created and tested will bring about this result. With the practice of these exercises you will experience the kind of harmony that shall make your path joyful and unending. You will learn how to save yourself and others, and how to live an eternal life.

Empowered by these concentration techniques and exercises you can always take active steps and exercise control in any situation instead of passively waiting for the outcome. Recognizing that the use of these concentration exercises in your everyday activities allows you to participate, in a very real way, in the process of universal salvation and eternal harmonious development, and lets you experience the freedom the Creator has given you. This is what shapes universal harmonious development alongside with your true personal wellbeing.

The concentration exercises and techniques are intended for 31 days. If you perform them in the month of February, which has only 28 days, then on the 1st of March you should move on to the exercise for the first day of the month. In other words, the day of the month from the list of exercises should always correspond to the calendar day. You may do the concentration exercises at any hour of the day. It is up to you to decide how many concentration exercises you want to perform per day and how long each one should take. It is useful to do the exercises on a routine basis as well as before important or stressful occasions.

If the first exercise of the day seems too complicated, you can skip it and practice the other two. You will still get results, and after a while the first exercises of the day will become easier to understand and simpler to carry out. So you don't have to force yourself: start by doing the exercises that you understand and like.

Let us now turn to the concentration exercises and techniques.

1st Day of the Month

1. On the first day of each month concentrate on the sole of the right foot.

This concentration technique connects you with the pivot in the world around you. In your mind, you are standing on the Earth, pressing against it with your legs and feet. The Earth acts as the supporting pillar in your consciousness.

Within the strategy for complete recovery, control is based upon the fact that this pivot has a dual function, i.e., that of support and creation. And since it also acts as the point of creation, you can simultaneously develop your consciousness with the help of these concentration techniques.

You begin to realize that just as everything on Earth, such as plants and even the tissues of your own body, grows and develops, in the same way you are able to build any external reality. Such understanding lies at the basis of this concentration technique.

Thinking about these deeper aspects during the exercise it is not an essential requirement, however. You can simply concentrate on the sole of your right foot and at the same time visualize the sought-after result in your consciousness. The principle according to which you are capable of building reality that I have just mentioned will be automatically engaged, and you will achieve the desired result in a harmonious manner, because this method of control is simultaneously responsible for creating harmonized events.

You can repeat this exercise several times a day.

2. Concentration on a seven-digit sequence of numbers: **1845421**; and then on a nine-digit sequence: **845132489**.

3. During this day you are supposed to concentrate on the World, on all objects in the World, and you should feel that every object in the World forms a part of your "Ego". As you begin to sense that, you will feel that a breath of wind from every object carries the hint of a solution. And after you begin to sense that every object in the World contains a part of your consciousness, you will experience the harmony which the Creator has bestowed upon us.

2nd Day of the Month

1. On this day concentration should be on the little finger of the right hand. As in the previous exercise, you must simultaneously keep in your consciousness the result you are seeking to achieve.

You are welcome to repeat this exercise several times a day with intervals which best suit your schedule. You may begin the new concentration exercise after a period of 20 seconds, or after an hour or more. You may perform the concentration once or twice daily, or ten times a day or more. It is also up to you to determine the length of each concentration session.

You should trust your gut feeling, your intuition. Learn to listen to your inner voice and to hear what it tells you. This applies to all of the exercises and techniques.

During this exercise you don't really have to remain absolutely still. You may even touch or feel something with the little finger of your right hand. You should be at ease and do what you like: it won't disrupt anything.

Here is what matters: in general, you have many sensing elements, of course. Apart from the little finger mentioned in this exercise there are nine other fingers and many other parts of the body. But at this particular moment you are being asked to select from this multitude of sensing elements and to concentrate only on one – namely on the little finger of your right hand. The purpose of this exercise is to harmonize your control of events. Your control becomes more harmonious.

2. Seven-digit sequence of numbers: **1853125**;
nine-digit sequence: **849995120**.

10

3. During the second day of the month you must see the harmony of the World in relation to you. You have to create the World the same way that it was done by the Creator. Look at the World and you will see the image of what was. Look at the World and you will see the image of what will be. Look at the World and you will see your own portrait showing what you now are in this World. This shall be the World everlasting and eternal.

3rd Day of the Month

1. On the 3rd day of the month the concentration should be placed on a flower or plant of your choice.

The plant can be physical – just as it exists in the real world around us. In this case, you can simply look at the plant during the concentration exercise. Or you can imagine the plant mentally and then focus upon the mental image of the visualized plant.

This concentration exercise resorts to the method of reflection. Here is the essence of this technique: while you are concentrating on the chosen plant, you imagine how your sought-after result is taking shape in the light that is reflected back from the plant. To be more precise, you don't merely imagine this desired result but you actually see it in front of you – you actually create this result.

An event that has been constructed with the help of this exercise becomes harmonized. The fact that the chosen plant already exists fairly harmoniously in the World also contributes to the success of this process.

2. Seven-digit sequence of numbers: **5142587**;
nine-digit sequence: **421954321**.

3. Look at the reality around you and you will see numerous worlds. Choose the world that you need, approach it and try to expand it. Look at this world with the eyes of an observer. Come close to it, place your hands on it, and feel the warmth that it gives off. Move this world closer to yourself and look at its Creator.

12

Listen to what He tells you and what advice He has for you. You can compare His knowledge to yours and so gain access to the World eternal and everlasting.

4th Day of the Month

1. On this day you should concentrate on crystals or stones. You can even use something as small as a grain of sand. Let's say you have chosen a particular stone. Now imagine a sphere around the stone as you are concentrating on it. This is the information sphere. In your mind's eye you can see how all the desired results become assembled within this sphere. You simply place the events you need inside this sphere. That is how control is being realized during the execution of this concentration technique.

2. Seven-digit sequence of numbers: **5194726**;
nine-digit sequence: **715043769**.

3. Use that aspect of reality which these techniques reveal to you. The techniques have to be harmonious. One method must follow out of the other, just as the second technique follows after the first. When you are walking down a street, you see that every new step arises out of the previous one. You can stand up from a sitting position and you take note of the fact that there are multiple possibilities for every movement. They may develop out of a previous movement and then they may themselves become the next previous movement.

Create the World as though it has always been a continuous entity and as if every movement of this World relates only to you as a unique person. When you create such an integrated World which will arm you with specific means of control in this World and through this World then, our World will exist everywhere and you will arrive there, and take it in your

14

hands, and your hands will become the World that provides support for your World. And you will see that you are able to touch the World eternal and everlasting, the World of Worlds. And it will be one and the same for everyone; it will be a unified World which you have chosen for yourself, as did everyone else. Create this World so that it is ideal for everyone and ideal for you. The ideal should not be divided. You should be able to see the ideal for all people – and yourself – in your unified World as well as in the unified World of all other people.

5th Day of the Month

1. On the fifth day of the month you should concentrate on those elements of reality that emerge as a result of your interaction with other elements of reality. Let me explain what this means:

When you direct your attention to any particular object, you in effect concentrate your consciousness on this object of reality. Through this connection with you, this object, this element of reality, acquires a certain portion of your concentration and a certain amount of your knowledge. This object then passes on to other elements of reality a part of the information it has received from you and some knowledge about your condition. In the same way, the light of the Sun shines upon various objects and is partially reflected, thereby illuminating other objects.

So after you turn to look at some object, following its interaction with you, this object will transmit something of itself to the environment. Your task therefore lies in contemplating this and figuring out what it is that each element of reality is passing on from itself to the environment. You can of course focus on just one aspect of this act. You may concentrate on the object while simultaneously imagining your desired result. This is the technique. What is special about it is that in this instance the desired goal is achieved through concentration upon the so-called secondary element, which you were able to identify.

Hence, with the help of logical thinking, with clairvoyance or any other spiritual pursuit, you identify exactly what the element you have chosen passes on to the environment after interacting with you. By con-

16

centrating upon this consequence, upon this secondary element of reality, while simultaneously visualizing the desired goal, you bring about its realization.

2. Seven-digit sequence of numbers: **1084321**;
nine-digit sequence: **194321054**.

3. When you look at the sky, you know that the Earth exists. When you look at the Earth, you may start thinking about the sky. When you are under the Earth, you know that the sky exists above it. These simple truths are the source of the World eternal and everlasting. Connect the sky with the Earth and you will see that everything that is under the Earth can also be above it. Walk towards your spirit, and you will find those who have been resurrected where they are to be found.

If you bring infinity to the truth of the World, you will see that the World is infinite. And when you know this, you will find the true, genuine Creator – the One who has given you what you have – and you will create as He has created. He is very close to you. He is your friend. He loves you. You only need to extend your arms towards Him and create as He does. You are His creation and you too are creators. Only the Creator, the Maker can create those who are creators. You should live in harmony with the Creator. You must be open before Him and you must be constant in all of your manifestations and in your own creations.

Everything you would like to correct can be corrected at any time. Everything you would like to create, you can create wherever you are – and at the time you choose for it. You have an eternity to attain perfection. For good deeds eternity is multiplied by the actions of the Creator. You are the one that He has seen in you and that He has created in you. But you are also the one who want the Creator to be represented forever in his deeds within the infinity in which you see yourself. The Creator that is present in you is the same Creator that works through you in each of your actions. Turn to Him and He will bring harmony into your life.

6th Day of the Month

1. On this day your concentration exercise should focus on changing the structure of your consciousness in the intensity of your concentration through the perception of distant objects.

This concentration technique is particularly useful when you would like the desired event to occur at a particular location. If that is the case, you need to concentrate the work of your consciousness precisely in these surroundings.

You can apply this technique just as successfully to accomplish the reverse: i.e., when you do not wish a particular event or situation to occur in a certain place, because it seems to you to be unfavorable. In this case you must disembody the negative information. Disembody means in this context to "unfocus" and "suppress" your consciousness in this location. The rarefaction that occurs as the result cancels out the unfavorable event or situation.

The realization of a desired event at a chosen location can be accomplished by concentrating upon distant elements within one's consciousness. We have already discussed this control technique before. In practicing it, you should use elements from your consciousness that are responsible for the perception of distant objects. In doing this, you can either look at actual physical objects, perceiving them with your normal eyesight, or you can visualize distant objects with your mind's eye. In both instances, you use distant elements within your consciousness. And when you simultaneously focus your consciousness on the event that you would like to see happening in a particular location, then it will occur in exactly that location.

19

The essential point in this technique is as follows: the more distant the areas of your consciousness where you deposit the information about your goal, the better it will be processed and the more complete the implementation of the event will be. And the event will occur at the chosen location.

When dealing with destructive forces you can use the "unfocusing technique". When you "unfocus" your consciousness, you can make the negative information rarefied to such an extent that it will no longer be perceived, as if it were not there in the first place.

2. Seven-digit sequence of numbers: **1954837**;
nine-digit sequence: **194321099**.

3. When you see the World as if it were somehow turned upside down, you must always remember that any upturned, disunited or compressed World is still the World of unity, harmony and grace. You must understand that God's blessing is inherent in all of the upturned, ambiguous or uncharacteristic conditions of the World. You can have access to this harmony, knowing that you have always been eternal, are eternal and always will be eternal. No misshapen structure or false information can change the Will of God.

7th Day of the Month

1. On the seventh day of the month you should concentrate upon the farthest reaches of your consciousness. We actually do this in our daily lives when we look at distant clouds or distant objects such as trees and their leaves.

In order to materialize a particular object or implement any desired event, it is necessary to process a large amount of information. The farthest reaches of our consciousness produce the fastest processing of information. The more distant the reaches of consciousness you choose, the faster the information processing you will be able to achieve.

The knowledge of these factors is used in this technique in the following way: you look at a cloud with your normal eyesight or see the cloud with your mind's eye and you simultaneously construct the desired event or sought-after result on this cloud (or, alternatively, on a leaf if you are looking at a distant leaf on a tree).

Through using the farthest reaches of your consciousness, you can quickly achieve the desired result, and the process of implementing the event will be harmonious, because the cloud cannot be an agent of destruction any more than the leaves can be. None of these objects of nature can cause anyone any harm, which allows the desired event to be realized in a harmonious manner.

2. Seven-digit sequence of numbers: **1485321**;
  nine-digit sequence: **991843288**.

3. You can see that the World develops in your image and according to the merit of your deeds in your interaction with God's Will. You see that the World is a creation that everyone accepts. And when you want to change the World through your actions, your deeds should be intended for the general good and then they will gain a foothold, your health will improve and the general good will be achieved. The general good is the deed of the World that leads you into God's Kingdom and to that state where you shall acquire a life, both universal and individual, eternally and forever.

8th Day of the Month

1. On this day you will learn how to exercise control while you are concentrating upon the consequences of events. Try to imagine yourself sitting by the lake, looking at a speeding motorboat. The water in front of the boat is quiet but behind it there are waves. The waves are a consequence of the boat's movement.

Let us look at a leaf growing on a tree. This leaf can also be viewed as a consequence of the existence of the tree.

Clouds gather and the first raindrops fall upon the Earth. The raindrops can be seen as a consequence of the existence of the clouds.

Similar examples can be found in great abundance around you. Take any phenomenon and concentrate upon one of the consequences it produces. While doing this, keep your desired event in your consciousness – and it will happen.

This control technique is very effective. With its help you can also change past events.

2. Seven-digit sequence of numbers: **1543218**;
nine-digit sequence: **984301267**.

3. You can see that the infinite curvature of the number 8 connects within it those Worlds, which you have encountered during the past seven days. And when you connect your World with all Worlds, you will become aware that you have as much joy in your soul as the World is diverse. If you perceive each particle of the World as an expression of general joy, you will see that joy is eternal, just as grace is eternal. Experiencing this general joy, you will raise your hands up to receive God's blessing which summons you into Eternity. See Eternity where it is. See Eternity where it is not. See Eternity where it has always been and you will become a creator of Eternity where it is not present from the point of view of others.

When you have seen Eternity and have created it, you will be forever eternal in everything, in any Eternity and in any World. You are a creator, in God's image and likeness, and Eternity creates you in His image and likeness. In creating Eternity you will create yourself. By creating yourself, you create Eternity, just as one Eternity can create another and as the Creator created everything at the same time.

9th Day of the Month

1. On the ninth day of the month you are going to take up the following task: concentration upon the farthest reaches of your consciousness brought to the closest areas of your consciousness. This means that the concentration involves transferring the farthest reaches of your consciousness into the closest ones. This transition must be carried out in such a way that your perception remains unchanged, whether it comes from the farthest reaches of your consciousness or the closest ones. This technique allows you to obtain a single unifying impulse for the creation of any element of the World. As soon as you can accomplish this, you will become a control expert. You will then only need to be in a certain spiritual state for everything to get back to normal. All you will need is to simply make a wish and things will happen precisely according to your wish.

The single unifying impulse of which I have spoken develops a particular spiritual state. This state does not have to be linked to any mental process, because your thoughts may not be involved in it at all. It may simply consist of an emotional inclination, for example, towards what is good, towards creation or the building of harmony.

The mere fact that this spiritual state contains such a positive inclination is already sufficient for the events to develop in a favorable direction.

I want to emphasize that this concentration technique identifies a particular form of perception. This perception within your consciousness represents a special area in it and you should try to structure it such a manner that it will function as I have described.

This concentration technique touches deeper aspects of exercising control based on the potential of your consciousness.

2. Seven-digit sequence of numbers: **1843210**;
nine-digit sequence: **918921452**.

3. When you understand the World is a very essential part of the creation of the Universe as a whole, you will see that everything and everyone that exists in nature, such as a plant, a human being, an animal, or a molecule, for example, everything that has not yet been created or else was created a long time ago – all of this has a single unified foundation from God Who has shown us the mechanism of all Creation. When you have seen how everything was created, you will be able to create any and everything yourself.

You can arrive at this level of cognition through the origins of your own "Ego". If you proceed from the depths of your "Ego", you will see how your "Ego" develops alongside with the entire Universe, how it grows and expands until it becomes transformed into the World. You are the World, you are reality. See this with the eyes of the entire World. Look at it with the eyes of every person, look at it with your own eyes and you will see that your soul is really your sight. Look at the World with your soul and you will see the World as it is and you will be able to make the improvements that are needed and you will see the World the way it should be for you to use it to attain life Eternal. You will always know the way when you look at the World from within yourself, from without, and from the outside – from all perspectives.

10th Day of the Month

1. On this day you should practice concentration based on the following technique: concentrate upon all of the objects of your external reality that you can apprehend simultaneously during a single impulse of perception.

You should prepare yourself to perceive in a single moment all of the objects that are available to your perception. As a result of this instantaneous act of perception, you should form an awareness of all of these external objects.

Of course, when you just start practicing this exercise, you are likely to obtain only a partial perception of the information about all of the objects. You needn't feel concerned. The complete perception of all the relevant information about all of the objects is the final goal of your work. With time you will develop such abilities.

Still, even when you start working on this exercise, the instantaneous perception of surrounding objects will permit you to gather at least some information from each object. You will have a general idea about the object and its location, for example, and you will know that such an object exists.

On the whole, in order to receive information about an object you basically only need to find the right place for concentration and to prepare yourself for the task. You will then be able to perceive any particular object and acquire access to all levels of control. And because this concentration technique teaches you to perceive a large number of objects simultaneously, this exercise allows you to control a large amount of information all at the same time.

27

Here is an example of the practical results achieved after the technique has been mastered: let's assume that there is a computer in front of you. As soon as you cast a glance at its external appearance, you immediately know how to use this computer and what one can expect to accomplish through its use.

The concentration exercise given here allows you to access information from any particular object since this technique will teach you to control any object of information. The access to the control of the information may be logical or intuitive, i.e., obtained at the spiritual level.

Summing up, I offered you a series of first exercises in concentration techniques for the initial ten days of the month. You could actually find other concentration techniques that you could use until the end of each month on your own. This could be done based on the cause-and-effect connections in the area of information. You could further develop what you already have, viewing the entire task from the position of fundamental control practices. Nevertheless, I have decided to continue the presentation of these concentration techniques, though I will make my descriptions somewhat more concise.

2. Seven-digit sequence of numbers: **1854312**;
nine-digit sequence: **894153210**.

3. The joining together of two numbers, the number one and the new number zero has led to you to see the World from the very beginning as though the number zero were already contained within the number one. When you observe the number one and increase it by tenfold through the addition of the number zero, what you have done constitutes an action. According to this principle, your actions and your deeds must be harmonious.

You must realize that your every action can expand any of your manifestations significantly, both in quantity and quality. You are the manifestation of the World. Create harmony between you and what you see. Pay attention to yourself and to your thoughts. You must be where you are. You must also be where you are not. You must be everywhere for you are the maker and the creator of all things. And your harmony must lead to Eternity.

Resurrection is an element of Eternity. Similarly, immortality is an element of Eternity. You must find the true Eternity for yourself where immortality and resurrection are only special manifestations of that Eternity. You must be the creator of each and every thing. You must figure out and form a precise picture of what follows after resurrection and immortality, after true immortality. True immortality initiates the next level of Eternity, the next level of the World and the next level of the personality. You must be prepared for this and always remember that new goals, the goals of Eternity, which were born before your time and which you have set for yourself, give birth to new Worlds that you build in your consciousness.

And this World, just as one and zero equals ten, this World is what you will always have when you become eternal, because you are already eternal. Your immortality is contained within you. You are already eternal and immortal – all you need is just to become aware of it. Ascend to this new level through a beneficial and reasonable action, similar to the joining together of one and zero, you will attain this immortality in all of your actions, in every manifestation and in every step you take.

11th Day of the Month

1. On the eleventh day of the month you should concentrate on the events that become manifested through the interaction of animals with humans.

Let us say there is a dog, for example, or a cat or some kind of bird, perhaps a parrot, living with you in your house. Contemplate the deeper meaning that underlies this contact, this interaction and communication with animals – from our point of view as well as theirs.

Becoming aware of the perceptions and thought processes of other participants in such interactions will allow you to enter the control structure in charge of our entire reality.

2. Seven-digit sequence of numbers: **1852348**;
nine-digit sequence: **561432001**.

3. Just like when you increased the number one by tenfold by adding the number zero to it, you get the next number when you add one to the number one. The number 11 is the embodiment of the World contained within you, which all can see. You are the essence that everyone can always see, and every person can have access to the harmonious experience, which was given to you in the process of your own development. Share your experience with others and you shall gain eternal life.

12th Day of the Month

1. On this day you should concentrate on those things where you could consider creating a whole, where something is missing. If, for instance, a goose or a swan loses a feather, concentrate on what one could do so that the feather returns to its place. How could you put it back? Try to understand how you could create a unified whole or how you could recreate something lost.

Or take another example: a leaf falls from a tree. What could you do to return the leaf to its former place so that the tree together with the leaf recovers its original state?

The purpose of this concentration technique is to teach you how to assemble separated elements of reality into a unified whole that represents their normal state. Practicing this exercise helps you to acquire control over events.

In this concentration session, as in many of the others, you can also take yourself as the object in the exercise. You can reconstitute any of your physical organs. A woman once came to me for advice. She underwent surgery during which her uterus had been removed. You can understand what that means to a woman. I used those very same principles and techniques that you have now learned, and this woman again has a properly functioning and healthy uterus.

2. Seven-digit sequence of numbers: **1854321**;
nine-digit sequence: **485321489**.

3. Unite with the World in its environment through your perception of

31

it in your own actions, and you will discover that your deeds are that very essence of the World, which is in harmony with you always and everywhere. You will see that God, when He gave you His blessing, desired to be one with you. You should find unity where the Lord is manifesting growth and development. In growth and development lies unity with the Lord. Unity arises in every moment of your progress during divine, genuine and creative growth and development. You progress and develop yourself in the direction of Eternity – this will forever manifest your unity with the Creator in your eternal growth and development.

You act and develop yourself in the direction of eternity and this, in your progress through eternity, will be forever your unity with the Creator. Life eternal and everlasting – that is the genuine, true unity with the Creator.

13th Day of the Month

1. On the thirteenth day of the month you should concentrate on certain individual, separate elements in a chosen object of reality.

Let us say you perceive some object, such as a truck, for instance, or a palm tree or a stone. It is doesn't really matter what kind of object it is. The main point here is that you consciously isolate certain elements or parts from the chosen object. When imagining a truck, for example, you can visualize it as being composed of many separate parts.

I should remind you that you can practice this technique on any form but never on a human being. You cannot work like this with people. A human being must always be perceived as a whole. This is the law.

However, if the object of your choice is not a person but something else, like the truck we mentioned before, you should be able to see it as being composed of a number of separate parts. Your task here is to find the connections that exist between the individual parts. When you discover these existing connections, while simultaneously keeping your desired result in your consciousness (such as the healing of some person, for instance, or acquiring the gift of clairvoyance), you ensure the materialization of this result. By using this technique you can perfect your ability to control real events.

2. Seven-digit sequence of numbers: **1538448**;
   nine-digit sequence: **154321915**.

3. You will see the faces of those who were involved in building this World before your time. You will see the tools by which this World was built before your time. You will see the World as it existed before you did. You will get the feeling that you were always present. Take this feeling and transfer it to the faces, and then use it to reconstruct these tools of Creation. You will become aware that the Creator is in everything around you, whether reproduced artificially or made by Nature.

He embodied you in everything you see. Your embodiment is expressed in the World that is presently being created.

This will help you to find any methods and techniques for your spiritual, intellectual, technological or any other type of development, so long as this development is creative in nature. Once you learn to interpret development as an equal universal process of development of any element of reality and any object of information you will discern that essence which is your own soul, your own personality and your Creator. The individuality of the Creator together with everything He has created lies at the foundation of World harmony. This harmony is inherent in everything; it is always present and always comprehensible.

The Creator Who has created you individually, as you alone, has simultaneously created everyone else. You should do the same by creating the World individually and at the same time for everybody, for all times and dimensions.

14th Day of the Month

1. On this day you should concentrate on the movement of the objects around you. Observe these objects and ask yourself: Why does this cloud move? What causes it to rain? Why can birds fly? Why do all these things happen? You should try to find the information content of all of these events.

If you concentrate in this manner and simultaneously keep your desired result in your consciousness, you will ensure that it occurs. At the same time you will improve your ability to control real events.

2. Seven-digit sequence of numbers: **5831421**;
nine-digit sequence: **999888776**.

3. On this day you should see your hands as hands that reflect the light of life. You should see your fingers as fingers that reflect the light of your hands. On this day you should view your body, as one which shines in the bright light of the Creator, shines with the bright light of love, goodness and health for all beings, and shines with the bright light of my Teaching on life eternal and everlasting.

On this day you can contemplate my Teaching on eternal life and address me in your thoughts. You can, of course, turn to me in your thoughts on any other day and in any other condition. You are always welcome to ask me for what you need for your eternal life and your creative efforts on behalf of all people. Turn to me and I will offer you my help.

You can, however, also turn to yourself and you will learn on your own what it is that you have received from me. You can experience this knowledge, use it and show it to others.

On this day you can be in harmony with me, just as you can harmonize with me on any other previous day and any other future day, if you wish. When time is no longer measured in the dimensions of time and space, you can always turn to me and always come to me for help, for a conversation, for an event you would like to see happen, or for anything else you would like me to be involved in.

You are free, as free as you always were. Consider this to be your law, spread this law around you and you will receive eternal life wherever I am. You will receive eternal life wherever you are and wherever everyone else is. You will receive eternal life where everyone is and that will be forever.

This principle will always be credible and true for everyone, for it already is credible and true for everyone. And you are the one who is in Eternity, for you are already Eternity itself.

15th Day of the Month

1. On the second day of the month you concentration technique focused upon the little finger of your right hand. On the fifteenth day you can practice this concentration exercise with a different part of your body, such as a different finger or a fingernail, etc., whatever you choose. In every other aspect, you should perform this concentration session just as I have specified for the second day.

2. Seven-digit sequence of numbers: **7788001**;
nine-digit sequence: **532145891**.

3. On this fifteenth day of the month you can experience that divine bliss, given to us by the Universal reason, which is thankful to the Lord for having created it. It is grateful for the creation of every one of its elements and for the creation of its high stature that enables it to reproduce the entire Universe because God is omnipresent.

In a similar fashion, you can also begin to experience the gratitude of the plants and the animals in relation to yourself, as well as the gratitude of other people and their love. You will see that you also feel love for them. Love is filled with creativity and benevolence, and it permeates all things. Universal love, which is within everyone's reach and which reaches everyone, this is the Creator, Who has embodied the World through your manifestation. You are the manifestation of the love of the Creator, because He exemplifies love in relation to you. You have received this gift of the Creator from the very beginning, and you are Him yourself – a creator – because you were created by Him, an all-encompassing, eternal and divine Maker and Creator.

You should go where He is – and he is everywhere. You should go wherever He calls you, since He calls you from everywhere. He is wherever you are and He is where you might be. You are in the movement of the Creator and the embodiment of His eternity. Follow in the footsteps of His deeds. He has created the World eternal in its universal development and interaction. You will see that the World is being created as eternal, and you will see that the World embodies you as eternal. You are a creator who has created all that is eternal. And the Creator has made you eternal in the creation of the World eternal and everlasting.

16th Day of the Month

1. On this day you should concentrate upon those elements of the external reality with which your body comes in contact.

As children we remember hearing praises sung to the Sun, the fresh air and the pure, cool water of a nearby lake. In this concentration session you should try to become aware of how you interact with these friendly elements.

Concentrate on the warmth, which the rays of the Sun bring you. You can feel their touch and sense their warmth.

You can feel the gentle breeze that caresses your body. You can feel its breath. It may also be a strong gust of wind or the still air of a hot summer day. And if it is very hot and humid, then you can feel the warmth, air and moisture on your cheeks all at the same time.

The refreshing effect of water can also be felt when you wash yourself, take a shower or go swimming.

This concentration exercise can also be performed during the cold months, since your face remains uncovered even in winter. And during the warm season, particularly in summer at the beach, your whole body can enjoy contact with the Sun, air and water. You can also add to this your contact with the Earth.

This exercise is extremely important because it involves conscious interaction with the elements of nature. You can, of course, practice this technique every day. If you keep your desired result in your consciousness while you practice this concentration exercise, you will ensure that it takes place.

2. Seven-digit sequence of numbers: **1843212**;
nine-digit sequence: **123567091**.

3. You should learn to feel harmony wherever it is, for it is everywhere and is always present there. It is the harmony of the Creator. Feel harmony where it is, where it was and will be. This is the harmony of your personal growth and development. Feel it where it is, where it was and will be and also where it was not, where it is not, but where it will always be. This is the harmony of change, the harmony of transformation. It is the harmony of the transformation into eternal life.

Come everywhere unto yourself, feel this harmony everywhere, and you will see how waves of love and joy emanate from your harmony. You will see that you are making the World harmonious forever in its permanent and eternal essence. You are a warrior, but you have now become a warrior enjoying God's eternal benevolence while you assure an eternal life and eternal faith.

17th Day of the Month

1. On the seventeenth day of the month you should concentrate on those elements of external reality that, from your own point of view, always surround you. These constitute the space around you, the Sun, the Moon, the constellations familiar to you and whatever else permanently exists in your image of the Universe. Concentrate on any one of these objects of reality and keep the desired result in your consciousness, as you always do, to ensure its realization.

2. Seven-digit sequence of numbers: **1045421**;
   nine-digit sequence: **891000111**.

3. Follow the resurrection of everything and everyone with your all-seeing eye, and you will discover that the reconstruction of the World is the reality in which you live. You will sense that you really exist in the eternal World. Move forward in this direction and you will see the path that calls to you. Take this path and you will see the Creator Who is eternal and you will delight in your eternity. And this delight is the eternity of life. And the Creator is the One, Who has created you.

His love is limitless and his humbleness inspires trust. He is humble and transparent, just as you have imagined, just as you have thought of Him before. He is just as benevolent and positive as you have already known before. He is your Creator and He shows you the way. Follow his path, because His path is your path too.

41

18th Day of the Month

1. On this day you should concentrate on stationary objects. These could be a building, a table or a tree. You may choose whatever object you like. Then try to figure out the individual essence of the chosen object, its meaning. We are talking about its meaning for specifically you. In other words, you need to understand what this particular object means for you. That is the purpose of this exercise.

From this point on, I will no longer include in the description of the exercise that, while you are concentrating, you must simultaneously keep the desired result in your consciousness to control its implementation. This will be assumed for the remaining exercises as well.

2. Seven-digit sequence of numbers: **1854212**;
   nine-digit sequence: **185321945**.

3. You should go where there are people. You should go where things are happening. You should work where there is resistance. And when you recognize this, the resistance will become transparent, its power will weaken and you will see the World of eternity even if there is still some resistance. Go and be wherever you want to be. You can be anywhere. You can embrace the entire World of wealth, and for this reason you fight with the resistance for an eternal life. The resistance falls. You will see the light of eternal life and receive it. So shall it be forever and ever, and for all times.

42

19th Day of the Month

1. On the nineteenth day you should concentrate on external phenomena, in which something that initially existed as a single whole then
became transformed into a sum total of individual parts. One example of
this is a storm cloud that becomes transformed into individual raindrops.
Another example is the crown of a tree that transforms into individual
falling leaves.

While you are concentrating on these or similar phenomena, try to
discover the laws, under which such a development of events can be
prevented. The purpose of this concentration exercise is to uncover such
laws.

2. Seven-digit sequence of numbers: **1254312**;
nine-digit sequence: **158431985**.

3. The struggle of the spirit for its rightful place in the World, as
well as the struggle of your soul for the embodiment of the Creator, results in your reason and your mind becoming controllable.
Your consciousness now belongs to everyone, and your portion
of consciousness becomes a part of universal consciousness. You
become what you are. Your Eternity is revealed in your reflec-
tions and your contemplations become Eternity. Your thoughts
make the World eternal. You will be where you are and you will
be where you are not, and you will be there forever, although the
World consists of intervals of time. And wherever you may be, an
interval of time will become the World, and space will unite with

43

Eternity. Time will retreat and you will be in movement and in eternal time. You will feel the eternal time and this eternal time will come to you. Every instant of your time is eternal. Feel the Eternity in every instant, and you will see that eternity is already part of your life.

20th Day of the Month

1. On this day you should concentrate on distant areas of your consciousness. Your task is to help other people.

Imagine that you have to explain something to another person, something that he doesn't know or else doesn't understand. Generally speaking, we know by now that in reality every person already possesses all existing knowledge, since everything is already in his soul from the outset. Therefore, your task consists of helping him to recognize the information that he already has inherently. Incidentally, true understanding is associated precisely with the ability to recognize knowledge that is already in your own soul.

The easiest way to achieve a person's awakening that makes it possible for him to recognize the necessary information, which is stored in his soul, is through the distant areas of his consciousness. Approaching this is most efficiently achieved through distant areas of your own consciousness.

By performing this exercise you are already actively participating in the program of salvation. In view of this, let me explain in greater detail what has to be crucial for your concentration effort. Your concentration technique must be performed in such a way that the control acquired by you would immediately lead to a positive and beneficial effect for everyone, so that a favorable development of events is simultaneously insured for everyone, irrespective of the actual location of the other people. They can be physically far away from you but will nonetheless receive your help.

In short, you could call this exercise a concentration technique to achieve general success. This means that thanks to your work will influence the development of specific events in the lives of all people in a favorable direction.

You may want to add another exercise on this day, particularly after you have just started working on this concentration technique. Concentrate on such distant objects like the Sun, the planets, or the stars and their constellations. You don't have to see them with your normal vision; your task is to try to recognize in your mind what these objects present from the point of view of information.

2. Seven-digit sequence of numbers: **1538416**;
nine-digit sequence: **891543219**.

3. Look at the World from the highest level of your consciousness, from the deepest recesses of your soul and with the strongest spiritual concern for the general wellbeing and prosperity. Look at the World as if it is still being created and create the World as it is now, but change the World's status quo, with its vices, in a positive direction, towards creation and eternal life. You will then see that what you thought were vices are actually a false understanding of the World. Understand the World correctly, the way the Creator has given it to you, and you will see that the Creator is everywhere and righteousness is everywhere. All you need to do is take a step in its direction, not denying its existence and moving towards this righteousness always and forever. Then you will see that the World has become transformed. And you will see that the Universe has becomes yours and that the Creator is pleased with you, and you will see that you are also a creator and can create everywhere and forever. You are a steward of the Creator and you also helper for all other people. Like

46

the Creator himself, you create the creator, and doing thus you arrive at the point where all are united.

This unity of all is your soul. Look at it and you will see the light of life. Your soul creates this light of life. The brilliance of your soul summons you to what is high up, what is wide and what is broad. The brilliance of your soul is the World. You see the World because your soul sees it. You see the soul because you have the eyes of the soul. Look at yourself from all sides, and you will see your overall unity with the whole World, with that entire World, which exists everywhere and always. Your thought is the thought of the World, and your knowledge is the knowledge of the World. Disseminate your knowledge of life, share the light of your soul, and you will see eternal life in the current condition of the World, where you find yourself. You will discover that eternal life has already been with you for a long time. Eternal life always is, always was and always will be. Eternal life is you.

21st Day of the Month

1. On the twenty first day of the month you should concentrate on numerical sequences that run backwards, for example: 16, 15, 14, 13, 12, 11, 10. The numbers presented in such a sequence must fall in the interval between 1 and 31 (the maximum number of days in a month). This gives you 31 numbers to work with. Trust your intuition in deciding what numbers you will chose for your sequence.

2. Seven-digit sequence of numbers: **8153517**;
nine-digit sequence: **589148542**.

3. Look at how a mountain stream runs down the mountain side. Look at the melting of snow. If you have seen these pictures with your normal vision, look at the images with your mind's eye. You will discover that your thoughts are no different than your eyes. You will realize that your consciousness is not different from your body, and you will see how your soul builds your body. Don't forget this knowledge, transfer it from one second to the next and share it with others. By creating Eternity out of the moment, you will build your own self eternally. It will be as though, without any special effort, you have lived before, and this eternal process of creation is what we call eternal life.

Construct other objects around yourself based on the same principle and build other worlds. Create joy, plant wheat and make the bread. Build new tools and machines, and make sure that the machines are not harmful and not destructive, and you will see that you live in this World, and it is given unto you, and that God and your own consciousness are

48

present in these machines. Stop the machines if they threaten you. Restore the body when it is ill. Put into effect resurrection when someone has departed. Do not permit the departure of another person. You are a creator and a maker – go and take action, and move forward in harmony with the entire World. Move in harmony with all Creation, in harmony with everything that will ever be created throughout eternity in all manifestations of the World, and in harmony with your own self.

22nd Day of the Month

1. On this day you should concentrate on elements of reality that are characterized by continual re-creation. One such example is the concept of Eternity, another is the concept of infinite space.

Let me remind you once again that while you are contemplating such concepts as Eternity and the like, you must simultaneously build your desired result and keep it in your consciousness.

2. Seven-digit sequence of numbers: **8153485**;
nine-digit sequence: **198516789**.

3. Your soul is a created structure; your soul is also a re-creatable structure. Look at how your soul is created and look at how it is re-created. Your soul is in the act of being re-created: uncover your World and see where the Creator re-created Himself. Look at the mechanism of such re-creation and you will see love. Love is what brings light into the World. Love is what the World is founded upon. Love has always existed and was there from the very beginning.

See the One Who created love and you will see yourself. The love that belongs to you is you who belong to love. Build with love, build with grace, build with the immense joy of all-encompassing life and mutual happiness for all, and you will be able to see the joy seen by all those who surround you. Learn to see the joy of all those who surround you and your heart will overflow with happiness. Be in happiness and harmony, and they will bring you Eternity.

Look with your eternal eyes at your family, look at them with your

50

eternal body, look at them with your eternal vision and give the gift of eternity to all who are dear to you. Look through your Eternity at all people and give them the gift of eternity. Look from within your Eternity at the entire World, at all those around you and give them eternal life. And the World will blossom, and a flower will appear that blooms eternally. This flower will be your World, which is also the World of all people. And you will live and your happiness will never end.

23rd Day of the Month

1. On the twenty third day of the month you should concentrate on developing all elements of reality to effect the ultimate realization of the divine purpose.

2. Seven-digit sequence of numbers: **8154574**;
nine-digit sequence: **581974321**.

3. Look at the World from the viewpoint of what needs to be done for it. Look at your own daily affairs, look at your feelings and examine them. See how your feelings are connected to life's events. Why do you look into the future, why do you feel a certain way, why do you take a specific course of action in your daily work? See why there is no place in the World for the word "alternately", because the World is unified and diverse in its unity. See why the word "unique" implies diversity.

Sense the nature of all things in your concrete affairs. Examine your own affairs from all sides. Look at your body and restore it to health with an instantaneous thought. Look at your consciousness and build it in such a way that it will resolve all of your problems. Look at your soul and realize that everything has already been here for a long time.

24th Day of the Month

1. On this day of the month your concentration exercise should focus on creating out of the human form some other object, for instance, a videotape, a pen, a flower or a plant. You should find out which element of the human form can be used to create a videotape, for example. In other words, how the human form should be interpreted in order to create a particular object, such as a videotape, out of it.

2. Seven-digit sequence of numbers: **5184325**;
nine-digit sequence: **189543210**.

3. You saw the reality you were able to see. You came to the reality that contains you. Look at all of the days, from the first to the twenty-fourth, and you will see that your love is endless. Look at the World the way you look at things with love; look at the feeling, at how you create it. Look at the feeling as something being eternally created and you will come to love as Eternity. You come to love always and you remain with it forever.

Your God, the Creator, has created you as a loving being. You are God's creation and you feel love. Love is life and life is love. Manifest your love wherever you are. Manifest your love in the places that you designate and that you predict. Love does not have to express itself in words, love may not be expressed in feelings, but your deeds wherever you are engaged in creating – this is love.

25th Day of the Month

1. On the twenty fifth day of the month you can concentrate on any object of your choice. What is important here is that you should perform a number of different concentration exercises so that you have some combination of these.

After an analysis of these selected concentration techniques you should combine various objects upon which you focused into groups, according to some general characteristic. For instance, you could place a tape recorder and a cassette into one group because they complement each other in their functions. A tape recorder and a radio could be designated to the same group when you view them as products that utilize electronics.

You can place similar objects, such as two different books, into the same group. However, if you view these books according to their subject matter or content, then these books could be designated to different groups if we use subject matter as the decisive criteria in our selection process.

As you see, you can give free rein to your imagination here. You can also stay at home and simply take a look around you, using these surrounding objects as the basis for this concentration exercise.

2. Seven-digit sequence of numbers: **1890000**;
nine-digit sequence: **012459999**.

3. Come to your thoughts about yourself inside yourself. Grasp the thoughts about yourself as your own reflection. See yourself in the same

54

way you see others. Look at yourself in the same way you look at everyone.

See yourself in the same way you see the branch of a tree, the leaf of a plant, the morning dew or the snow on your windowsill. You will see what is eternally before you. You will see that you are eternal.

26th Day of the Month

1. On this day of the month you will learn simultaneously to see the whole and its parts, the general and the specific.

Let's say there is a herd of cows in front of you. You can see the entire herd and at the same time you can concentrate your attention on a single cow. You can simultaneously try to understand what this particular cow is thinking and how it will develop in the future. In the same way you could observe an entire anthill and simultaneously concentrate you attention on a single ant.

With the help of this concentration technique you should learn how to see the whole and its part, the general and the specific practically in one glance. This exercise helps you to develop this ability. You will be able to see the whole and its components simultaneously.

2. Seven-digit sequence of numbers: **1584321**;
nine-digit sequence: **485617891**.

3. Take into account the fact that you are continually developing. You should see that your development is a continuous, uninterrupted process. Occupy yourself with that which is eternal, for every action is eternal, every object is an embodiment of Eternity, every individual is Eternity and every soul is a multitude of Eternities. Go from a single unified Eternity to diverse Eternities and you will see that there is only one Eternity for everyone. Come to an insight into your soul through this, and you will see that you are the creator of whatever you need.

Use this knowledge for the creation of each individual object, and

56

you will see that each individual object has been created by you. Use this knowledge for the creation of your body, and you will understand that your body can restore itself at any time. Use this knowledge to recover the health of others, and their healing will give you additional experience. The healing of others always gives you personal experience. Re-creation of anything always gives you additional experience.

Do more good, bring more joy and happiness and you will receive the gift of Eternity in the form of a concrete technological tool of your consciousness. Expand your consciousness to satisfy the harsh requirements of Eternity. And wherever Eternity is expanding, overtake it. Overtake Eternity within infinity and see yourself as the embodiment of the Creator. Create where Eternity is just beginning to expand. You are the creator of Eternity, you control Eternity, and Eternity will obey you always and forever.

27th Day of the Month

1. On the twenty seventh day of the month you should perform the same concentration exercise that you did on the ninth day, adding to it such a feature as the continuous, uninterrupted development of each element that you are focusing on.

2. Seven-digit sequence of numbers: **1854342**;
nine-digit sequence: **185431201**.

3. Help those who need help and help those who don't need any help. Help yourself when you need help and help yourself when you don't need any help. Reflect on the word "help" in its broadest definition and reflect on "kindness" as the manifestation of help. You are a kind human being, which is why you help others. You are a creator, and you have the ability to help. Every act of your creation also brings help to you. Everything that you have created also helps you. You have an infinite number of helpers just as you help an infinite number of other people.

You have universal connections with everyone: you always help everyone and everyone always helps you. Bring society to a state of well-being and prosperity through your universal connections with everyone and mutual help, give happiness to all and you will find yourself in a state of general, universal harmony with all others, where God the Creator is everything that has been created around you. It is everything that you have created and the embodiment of God in everything that has been created around you.

And after you receive eternal life, the embodiment of God as your

58

Creator will be manifested in your soul as a genuine understanding of the World in its self-development. The eternity of life is the eternity of the Creator. To be able to live forever, one must forever be created and one must forever be re-created. You don't need to do anything in particular in order to be created forever, for we were already created for Eternity to be forever re-created. You are capable of making every one of your thoughts, every one of your movements, and every one of your deeds create Eternity.

28th Day of the Month

1. On this day of the month you should perform the same concentration exercise that you did on the eighth day but with the following important distinction: you have probably noticed that on the previous day, the 27th day of the month, when you performed the concentration exercise in a certain way, the numbers 2 and 7 were added together: 2 + 7 = 9. In this instance the situation is different: the number 28 contains the numbers 2 and 8. Here you should multiply two by eight. In this case the eight is doubled, which is precisely why the exercise from day eight is repeated.

However, this repetition should not be automatic; it should not be an exact copy of your previous work. You must change something and the change must primarily affect something within yourself, for example, your vision of this particular concentration technique. While performing the exercise according to the former technique, you should find something new in it and view it from a different angle.

Your understanding and perception of this concentration exercise should expand and deepen continually. This is a creative process that furthers your development.

2. Seven-digit sequence of numbers: **1854512**;
nine-digit sequence: **195814210**.

3. Look at yourself the same way that you see the entire World all at the same time. Look at the Creator the same way that the Creator sees you and acquire through this an understanding of what the Creator wants from you. Look at His gaze and you will see His gaze. You will see that the Creator's gaze is also directed towards the distant phenomena of the World. It is your goal to learn how to control these phenomena. You must make any phenomena of the World harmonious. This is your true goal.

You must initiate and create Worlds that will always be harmonious. And this is your true mission from the way you have been created. He, the Creator, has already created and He, the Creator, has already made it, and your goal is to follow this path, because you have been created in the image and likeness, just as the Creator himself was created.

The Creator has created Himself, but He has also created you. Create yourself and create others. Create all others and give them universal wellbeing and prosperity, and you will have the World that was created for you, for all and for the Creator. Create for the Creator, for He has created you. Create for the Creator, for he has created everything. And this is why anything you might, you always create for Him.

29th Day of the Month

1. On the twenty ninth day of the month you should perform a summarizing concentration exercise. On this day you are expected to review all of the exercises from the first to the twenty eighth day. But you must perceive them as a single impulse. This is very important. You should grasp the path that you have covered during the entire month in a single instant of perception.

In doing this, you should subject your work to a certain analysis. This is the day when you create something like a platform for your next month's work. You can visualize everything you have done in the form of a sphere and then place this sphere on an infinite straight line whose starting stretch extends into the next month. Hence, you will create not only a platform for the next month, but also for your eternal continuous development.

2. Seven-digit sequence of numbers: **1852142**;
nine-digit sequence: **512942180**.

3. Look at the World with your own eyes. Look at the World with all of your feelings. Look at the World with all the cells of your body. Look at the World with your entire body and with everything with which you are able to see and everything that you are. Look at the World and at yourself, and look within yourself. Look at the World with the understanding that the World is all around you, that it envelops you. Look at the reality that grants you life. Look at the reality that has granted you Eternity. You will then see that wherever you should look there is no other reality but this one that grants you life and grants you Eternity.

God is the Creator of this reality. And God, Who created this reality, also created eternal life. He sees you as you see yourself, and He sees you as you don't see yourself. He is your Creator. He is God.

30th Day of the Month

1. On this day you should perform your first concentration exercise based on the platform which you have constructed. This concentration session creates the groundwork for your work during the next month.

Concentrate on the harmony of the World. You have to see it, discover it, enjoy it and admire it. At the same time you can't help being amazed at how perfect the Creator has made everything. In other words, you admire the harmony of the World, which is explained by the perfection of the Creator.

2. Seven-digit sequence of numbers: **1852143**;
nine-digit sequence: **185219351**.

3. The principle according to which the exercises of all of the previous days were constructed may on this day be considered fundamental, because in February, which, according to the current calendar has 28 or 29 days, this principle is transferred on the thirtieth day to the first or the second day of the following month. This unification manifests the eternal cycle of life. Discover Eternity in all of your previous techniques aimed at achieving harmony.

Find Eternity in this simple example, where one month has 30 days, while another, February, has 28 or 29 days, and only through this one month February we have the unity of the number 30 with the numbers 1 or 2. And the unity of numbers that are different in nature and in origin is an expression of the unity and common origin of all things. Find this common origin in everything, in every element of information, in places where it is not immediately apparent and where it is obvious, and where it can be seen immediately. And you will see, you will comprehend, you will feel, and this will elevate you spiritually.

31st Day of the Month

1. On the thirty first day of the month you should concentrate on the isolated areas of any particular volume.

Let's imagine that there is a tree growing on some plot of land. You realize that under the tree is the earth, and that above and around it is the air. All of these separate areas come together in your consciousness because of the fact that you see in all of them the eternal re-creation of life. Life is eternal – you should recognize this. Remember it while you are observing the surrounding World, while you are experiencing it and becoming immersed in it. And the recognition of this truth will come to you: YES, INDEED, LIFE IS ETERNAL.

2. Seven-digit sequence of numbers: **1532106**;
nine-digit sequence: **185214321**.

3. Concentrate upon yourself on this day. You are absolutely and completely healthy, and everyone around you is healthy as well. The World is eternal. All events in life are creative in their nature. Always see everything in a positive light, and everything around you will always develop in a favorable direction.

I would like to add a few more comments to the proposed series of exercises. Let me remind you once again that you determine yourself the number and length of the concentration sessions. It is also up to you to decide, what result is the most important for you to achieve in any given moment, what you are primarily striving to accomplish. When you wish to obtain a desired result by a particular date, add this time to the set goal and try to achieve it through your concentration techniques.

Remember that all of the exercises are creative in nature. They will assist you in your further personal growth and development. With the help of these exercises, you will grow spiritually, and this will help you perform them at a higher level in the future, guaranteeing your continued development ad infinitum. Quite soon you will notice that your life has begun to change for the better. To be more precise, however, it must be said that you yourself have started to improve it, that you have begun to take control of your life.

These techniques and exercises will develop your consciousness; they will influence the direction of your life's events in a positive way; and they will help you achieve perfect health and be in tune with the pulse of the Universe.

Notes

Notes

GRIGORI GRABOVOI

CONCENTRATION EXERCISES

EDITION 2011-1,23.12.2011

ISBN: 978-3-943110-31-9

CPSIA information can be obtained at www.ICGtesting.com
Printed in the USA
LVOW120057270213

321795LV00001B/347/P